# PUNCHLINE

Whitney —
    For all our unravelings,
  for all our beauty —

# PUNCHLINE
## Nick Courtright

3-2014

**GOLD Wake Press**

Boston, Massachusetts

Published by Gold Wake Press
& J. Michael Wahlgren

Cover design by Justin Runge
www.justinrunge.me

ISBN 10: 0983700125
ISBN 13: 978-0-9837001-2-8

Pre-publication excerpts from this book
appeared on CultureMap Austin
austin.culturemap.com

Punchline
2012, Nick Courtright

www.goldwakepress.org

for my family

# Contents

The Despot                                    3

## ...He does not throw dice"

He Does Not Throw Dice                        13
Memory                                        15
The Present                                    16
The Garden                                     17
What We Know and What We Don't                18
Query                                         19
Regret                                        20
What I Have to Say to You                      21

## ...Invent the universe"

Invent the Universe                           25
The Revision Process                          26
Fun with Agnosticism                          27
Dogma                                         30
The Apocalypse                                31
Consolation Prize                             32
What Is                                       33
Freedom Evolves                               34
Eternity at the All Night Diner               36
As If We are All Immigrants                   37
No Children                                    38
Gulf                                          40
Journey to the Bottom of the Sea             41

# ...Worry to die"

| | |
|---|---|
| Worry to Die | 47 |
| Congruence | 48 |
| Faith | 49 |
| Where am I Going, What Have I Been | 50 |
| Illumination and Darkening | 52 |
| Urban Tapestry | 54 |
| Phenomena | 56 |
| Poverty | 57 |
| The Liberation of Tibet | 58 |
| American Conundrum | 59 |
| Steel Country | 61 |

# ...Nothing special"

| | |
|---|---|
| Nothing Special | 65 |
| Reluctant Prophet | 66 |
| Wake | 69 |
| Fatalist Theme Song | 70 |
| Ghosts | 71 |
| Connection | 73 |
| Punchline | 74 |
| Mosquito | 76 |

A drawing of the moon:

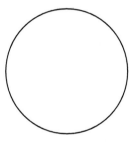

# The Despot

*~ a preface*

I.


The streets down and nights through

which the despot wanders,
dressed in pajamas

making his selections, these are the streets everyone knows

we cannot trust.
Because who can you trust?

Imagine all the guitars in one pile,

one of fire and strings and wooden boxes—
the strings, do they play

for the heat

or do they lay dormant, shapeshifting
into the unmemorable,

into songs we cannot hear, as if we were children, deaf—


•

imagine one of them, one of us
seeing

if maybe he got close enough

he would be able
to make out the song of the robin, red-breasted.

He, *us*, is trying to hear the birdsong.

Imagine the boy
just before he fired the small gun

he couldn't hear,

laying out the soundless bird
before him.


•


He wrote every mercy he could think of, Lord have mercy,

God have mercy,
let me please have mercy

for all things and remember

the ant
could conquer this planet

if only she were larger.

4

II.


You know like omniscient monks know, as one recalled
the dream you had of your mother

on the night she died—

half a world away she died
and the other half of the world away

you dreamt

and another half yet
the monk knew and wept.

A true monk accepts the beauty of all things,

yet has compassion for those who suffer
the things we, in our human way, deem sufferable.


              •


He sees a bird nearby

as he sits on the shoulder of a hill
and he hears it, he would have to hear it

even if deaf, because to be omniscient is to know

even what you cannot
know.  Anything less

5

would make him, again, in his loincloth, just a man.


•


Because of all this the monk
would not think

to kill the bird and learn the lesson, because killing,

although without flaw
and wholly of the absolute's nature,

is to bring about the judgment

between suffering and not suffering, and to make real
the division of choice,

even as division itself is glory, and to learn a lesson

is excess, is the path to wisdom.
But what can be of the path when it has

already been learned,

was learned before you were born,
you, monk, you, ant who makes hills like sand?

III.


Humans

use sand to make glass,
through which we see to the other side,

and to make computer chips,

with which we store our knowledge, and gain more of it,
and seek the face of God

and find it

on the internet.  Maybe
the face of God was always there, in the sand itself,

and the ant had access to it,

knowing truth
one organized plan at a time,

and has conquered in its own way, reigning

miniature terror
over fields like women and men...

Let's in these ways be careful not to get carried away.

IV.

You, earth of utter simplicity, but only
in its and our imagination

where we are kings, when you are on the mountain

making your hike to that swimming hole
where you can only hope

your true love waits—

*It would be the closest the world had seen to a perfect love. For the first time an example that two people, two different entities, had truly acted as one. It's almost impossible to consider because two human beings are not so much like two lamps, who together light a room with one light so that you can see the fineness of hair, but that two human beings could be an organism of their own and have the unified good, that their moral love would be what was good for them each, and that the cries at the end of a phone call for the loss of yet another thing mean there's so little to do, because the pity of one's self is the pity of everything—*

You are still hiking, your boots are wet

from having crossed a river
some time back, and now you are on your way up.

Look: you're proxy

for me, and for you, and for you and for us,
and for the stone, and the cat

# He Does Not Throw Dice

Imagine the lawlessness
of the subatomic world, but larger.
Then imagine that the lawlessness present there
is in fact lawful, that there is no such thing
as lawlessness, that even
the apparently most random event
is wholly predictable
by a system that takes into account
variables we cannot take into account, so short
is our attention span
in regards to the unseen, or the unseeable.
Like Wright, you could say
that something has been wasted, been washed away,
that the night is a cell
from which you compose your last notes
with the pen a sympathetic guard
passed to you through the bars, that when they take
his head
it'll be yours in the basket
he thinks of second to last. Last,
that'd be his own head in the basket, because regret
and maybe even vengeance surely
could not be the last thought,
because the way you lived is the way
you end, and that is, *alive.*
Right?

...Make a pale blue map of your day in the grass,
when you are just
the drink the drunks have awaited.

# Memory

History could end,
it could be replaced

with myth. It could be revised by pamphlets fallen

from the sky, or Adobe Photoshop.

Maybe history was never there at all

and in the telling
we feigned objectivity or honesty. Or it wasn't feigning

necessarily
but a lack of insight

into the impossibility of telling
a story the way the story happened:

we couldn't count all the faces in the subway station,
for example,
all of them

destined to be just a bit shy of exact, in the lie of text.

# The Present

*: you don't mind it*
*when you don't mind it*
*and you do when you do :*


Careening dragonfly-like

towards the unknowable, ashes to non-ashes to ashes—
you never know

what you'll become
in five thousand years' time.

To be the hindquarters of the new
dinosaur, or the lantern of a disciple

mining the soil for his granddaughter's remains.

Two futures that could be yours.  You could have both.


*Chances are    Chances are    Chances are*
*you will.*

# The Garden

It is all this material stuff.  It is a deer

leaping over a white picket fence, its fawn in tow.


So bless


the tearful rush of falling,

and sing each of these seeds
into its bed—


I may have thirteen explanations

for every way
we've failed,

but I know no explanation for the thirteen explanations.

# What We Know and What We Don't

The ceiling fan whose arms
are shifting ghosts
of wind,

or the litany of constellations

whispering down to the hood of a car on which two teens
lay—

they are not as solid as you think they are
and neither are you.


Give in to this and you can be

just a star.  That's what they whisper, they have been
all along,

but only special radios can hear,

like a whistle for calling dogs, calling them home.

# Query

The wind is not a thing on its own, it is just air, moving.

I think that's what Aristotle would say—


that air is the substance, and wind
merely a condition of air, and therefore
not a substance of its own.  That's the safe bet


but any honest person
would have to wonder

what if wind is the substance and air is wind afflicted
by stillness?

# Regret

To call a fire alive, to call a ghost awake,
to call a ghost asleep, or to call it on the phone,

pressing redial one two three
four twelve twenty-one times
and always being sent to voicemail.  It's your first love

again, and it lives.


At what point does the fire die,
does the ghost pick up the phone and whisper

*I knew you'd keep calling*
*until I answered, so now I've answered, what is it you*
*have to say to me?*

# Invent the Universe

In the bottom of the well:
that's where we'll stay.  In there it's dark and if not

for the blind man who passes
daily we would

have no one at all.  Lucky for us

he threw
that coconut down, down

the well and now for fun we just have to get
the damn thing open...

# The Revision Process

In a perfect
vision of how our solar system story went,

the plot should have been drawn out

just a little more, and we should skip
that part in the middle

that didn't make any sense—

let us get to the end
where we were meant to be from the beginning.


Yes, take out

the atom
and the deity routine

all flash and jazz, the impotent

feelings of the defeated, the part about the victor striding...

# Fun with Agnosticism

Say God made a dinosaur

so as to kill the dinosaur, and all the other dinosaurs,

his terrors of the sky summoned,
the great lizards compelled to halt their telepathy,

those who lived
relocating to different planets or far underground—

about all this deified lifetime's debris,
it's not right

to chitchat.


&bull;


As we crawl through our tunnels and weep

*it's just a mystery*

we should at least have fun with it,
we should set 'em up and knock 'em down, time after time

until our singing voices are raw

and riders

on their bicycles

flash like swallows through red lights, taking risks
with space and the laws of motion—

their souls are Las Vegas and their bodies are casinos,

and it's just one dice roll, then another.


•


Let's let us believe
it's not a mystery but only probability,

and all the ratios are undefined.  Pull down the blinds
and be the darkness

you wish to see in the world,

your obscurities
shaken into focus by a swarm of ambiguity,

the definition of one string of letters begging

for more strings of letters

sorting out their definitions.  But that too is okay!


•

Our chasing of the tails we're attached to

is a good time, if dizzying,
and we can make some sense of it.  If we're lucky,

from above,
if we move fast enough

it seems our tireless, circuitous blur

is a perfect circle.

# Dogma

Dogma, from the Greek, means "that which one

thinks is true,"

but less literally, and less terribly,
it just means opinion. We've been advised

to shy from it.

I picture this: a dog barking, but its bark
is insistent

and all the shouts
out the window at it to

*quiet the hell down*

won't get the job done.

This is dogma
I'm talking about, so watch out.

It'll keep you up at night, and if it doesn't then maybe
you've lost your hearing.

# The Apocalypse

A slew of frogs, a battalion, an army,

all the vultures and octopi under attack,

the headless bodies of octopi
and bodiless vultures' beaks blood-masked

until, eventually, it becomes clear the birds had eaten
their own bodies
and the heads of the octopi

and then something even weirder
happens, two thousand earthworms
flying through the sky, polar bears driving cars, et cetera.

—At that we will know
what we have wrought
is upon us.

# Consolation Prize

The moon would be within a step

if we were eighty trillion times the size we are, just like Florida
is far from Cuba for the man who swims there.


After the flood we'll all be heroes, if we're left.


The new survival of the fittest

will be the best swimmers, meaning especially webbed fingers and toes
will be cherished and sought after
in the new breeding prioritizations of humanity.


Bees are dying off, like dinosaurs, and someday we'll all go.

# What Is

Apocrypha is no less than actual, if it is believed.


And apostle is no less than prophet,
if the apostle's prophet is true, and the latter is false.


All the world is a sad place if you say so.


During each moment that could
become truth, what is abandonment, what is traitor?


What would it cost to be Benedict Arnold?


In your mouth, each blessed addiction
like a horse pill stuck in a grandmother's throat,


stepping back into the kitchen, hearing not one siren.

# Freedom Evolves

You sat outside the old house and there

learned of paint
and shelter and the meanings of roofs

when they reveal their feelings about being

shield against the rain, a protector.


•


Now the sky is a wide cloth above

and the moment outside
has become me.  It will rain so hard

the whole idea of wet will change—

we are all being waited for, we are all the analogy.


•


You believe in free will

and then one day so does

one atom of the gum-covered underbelly
of a forty year old desk

and who is affecting who?

•

Maybe that one atom is as responsible
for the whole room around it

as a human is for the galaxy, the awful galaxy.

In that case, slow down,

little everything.

# Eternity at the All Night Diner

The friend who gave me the I Ching
said she could channel electricity

and though that may be possible

staring so intently at the outlet won't make it happen.

At least I wouldn't think so.


Still, I would dream
of her fingertips,

the electricity shooting from them.


But no matter how much coffee I drank

I never became coffee, and flipping coins
to determine the best route to decision-making
is just a way to find

a page.  That's how the I Ching works.


But it helped: I am here.  I am here instead of there.

# As If We are All Immigrants

If we are honest, not one of us has remained
where we were born.  Nor did

the human race stay tied
to its origin: it spread out.
Like fog

it climbed into the valleys,
and was a halo around the skulls of mountains.


                        Or,

for us to make homes
we all have lost our mothers,

we all have become our fathers, even those
who've never
known them—

in time we will wash our hands in change,
we will be the thin rivers of a barren landscape.



                        Or,

like the last droplets of sunlight

smoldering the edges of the highway,

soldering it
with the handprint
of heat

so that it will buckle and tire
when the heat is gone, we too have left our sun.

# No Children

If Heaven
is so blissfully


lonely
let me have


none of it.

# Gulf

We are all ghosts
too shy to break

from the shadows, huddled there in fear of being
discovered, playing gently our silent

electric guitars
for an audience of the knowing animals.


Dust motes have become
our best friends, how

they seem to waft up, defying gravity, every now and then
despite the absence of wind.


Perhaps our breath ricochets
forever until it is the burning

of the bottoms of our feet on the surface of the sun,
or on the hot sand

of the beaches of our childhood, where we could not
run fast enough to the water.

# Journey to the Bottom of the Sea

The feel of coolness around you, to make your way into it

in a child's strides
against the waves

rolling like patterns of awake and asleep

until the water is past your midsection
then your chest

then your feet can no longer touch

then you are alone for the first time, ocean on all sides of you
and it always had to be this way

•

to no longer see land,

to feel yourself an individual. If only the panic of your insides
and the panic in your eyes

surveying the blankness of endless water

could be quelled, it would be possible to find peace, to stop
kicking to stay above,

to allow the sinking two miles to the bottom,

to discover the Lusitania and all the other great ships
mankind could not make unsinkable—

·

you could swim their corridors

and magnificent ballrooms
eavesdropping on the conversations of sharks

over cocktails.

You could play cards
with the grand octopus

whose idiot face has a wisdom all its own, though of course

he'd win, if only because he could play
so many hands at once. *Please let me win just one time.*

·

Eventually, moving on would be necessary,

to admit the mistakes of the salacious
anemone, the mistakes

of the twentieth century and the nineteenth

century and this century and all the other centuries as well,
la la la. Soon, digging

would be destiny, digging beneath the surface of the sea bed, soft

at first and then hard, through the alien
outcroppings in which the deep-down animals hide,

•

their eyes narrowing

upon you as you dig, down, down, the hole filling with water,
then with sweat, then with heat.

—And the possession most cherished in this exploration

would be a surprise considering at some point
faith was that possession:

apparently, the correct answer all along

was a good flashlight, to find
your way through the darkness that seems to, or does never, end.

# …Worry to die"

"As I have not worried to be born, I do not…

~Federico Garcia Lorca, in an interview, 1936

# Worry to Die

Eventually progress has to come, lest we be buried
in unmarked graves.

Generations later, they'll try to exhume us
but all their digging

will turn up nothing—

how many millions of light years must we travel

before we realize
we are all just snakes' tails
in the mouths of snakes?

# Congruence

It is like the Dalai Lama
wandering with humility

through the terrible corn of Iowa, intoning
*I am so lazy, I am so lazy*

and meaning it
despite its obvious untruth in comparison

to the doings of others
for whom even love is a challenge.


They have so much to say
and so few ways to say it.


Like the stars which vanish above tonight's
big city, become something

invisible to you now, but visible later, much later,
when you have left

this present, when all the differences
between acorn and oak have faded away.

# Faith

The workers
who crafted pyramids

out of the sand, rose them up
under the hot sun and the narrowness of the Nile,

what did they say to themselves
when honored, when they were sealed

within the walls, when the air began to thin?


Maybe

*I will be here*
*with the pharaoh, here*

*with the gods, only Ra*
*cannot see me now.*  And five thousand years later


Dear Museum, make it gentle, my brittle fingers bent,
hands clutched in pagan

beggar divine renunciate
prayer.

# Where am I Going, What Have I Been

When I was young
I said I did not care

what became of my body but I wanted

the monument honoring me
to be massive.  And now that I am older

maybe the truth is that I wish
for the monument to remain, but the body as well.


I would like to know
where it is, and to have it taken care of

because, Dark Lord of the Unanswered,

it is my future, the one I can count on most,

this cathedral of parts.


Father Whitman made a point

to note how we shall become
grass,

and the grass shall become us.  In others words,
remember:

with enough time


*grass to grass, stone to stone, myth to myth.*

# Illumination and Darkening

When the fires retrieve their damages
from within themselves,

wishing they could

take back a thing or two

they said,
the rose of discarded friendship—


what each petal represented
when it represented

what you did not desire, the contemplation

of true love
on the hour of your first death—you made it


after CPR but for a moment

you were gone.  What did you see?


It's not what I saw, you said, it's what I felt.

And what did you feel? Nothing.

# Urban Tapestry

The city was alive with
the lanterns we all are

when held up to a bright enough light.

If fortune and past lives smile upon us, everyone will rest easy.


•


And like the body of a small dog

I was a transformation of gravestones
into children.  It seemed an inevitability I would be this.


Transformation this, transformation that.  This will occur.


Who knows what fallacy
we'll engrave after we're saved.

Slippery slope?  Straw man?  Red herring?


•

About you
a woven blanket and beads

native children sold on the sides of dirt roads

between one place and another, not like other histories
so many uses had crossed out.


By the time I die I'd like to know if enlightenment is real.


•


In the city, left and right and up and down are more than ideas,

and the walls,
I would call them paper thin but this was thinner:

the apse of consciousness

like an award
at the depths of the day—


•


you never know
what's trapped

in the minds of
the silent

# Phenomena

Often, in a dream
all the moose
will wander as they do and one can only do so much.


Gasoline for Hell and lawnmower, respectively.


And the inexplicable moose,

that wanderer without a want
who spends his nights
like the verb
suggests; forever, on the brink.


Don't let the lover's driven heart
take names, or make your name
into one body
tottering over the edge.

The deceased are only as alone
as they want to be, as we want them to be, and vice versa.

# Poverty

The water is no longer water, it's still as death,
still as a dead tree
or a photograph of lightning

like an old woman's veins across the electric sky.

This lightning is for all eternity

or until the decomposition of the photo paper

striking the farmhouse
to take it down

into elemental burning,
everlasting destruction

made firm by capture.  Is the captor human or film?

It doesn't matter, we are all the water, frozen.

Now let's say there is

no water, and you, poverty, in your stillness
are lightning.

# The Liberation of Tibet

Once, there was the question of luck, if it is a plant

I can water: this is my luck plant, and if I tend to it
I shall be rewarded, if it receives sun
it will blossom into opportunity,

or if luck is not a plant: it cannot grow, it cannot be watered

and if you have it
you do, and if you don't
you don't.

•

In a way, it's like scaling the walls

of an abandoned industrial paradise.  Pipes, nitrogen oxide,

all rust and grease embedded in prayers

deep in the skin of His non-seeking hands.

# American Conundrum

State boards of education across the U.S.
pretend it is

1830 and in 1830,
it turns out, was passed into law

the Indian Removal Act, the beginning of the end
for the possibility of

nation within nation
within the United States, and yet another challenge

for the twenty-first century
citizen's patriotism.


•


How many stars can you count
lying on your back

or on the rooftop of a temple or Target?
Chances are you can see

more than you can count, not necessarily because
you cannot count that high

but because you cannot well enough

keep track. But even if you could count that high

and keep track, that wouldn't be sufficient.
There are just too many.


•


These are the issues, among people, that drive people
to drink. But don't blame them,

the stars, the people, the people, the drink.
Praise them all,

the eyes of the beach, the wreck and relic of ships split
upon the dying shore,

the many mistakes our sea to sea has made and will make.
Bless them, and say hello, Americans,

where are your souls,
your souls are here.

# Steel Country

It came late to the party like rain
after the drought, that dry year
sealing the deal for this landscape, its flatness

murmuring *mothball* in a ceaseless susurrus:


we all know what happens,

the progress of evolution, the still hard

dry dust-covered non-progress
of evolution.  Like one season into the next

it's never truly going anywhere.


Like desperate child wishes

said to the stars above the campground,
take your own heart, see

what it's made of, what it pumps, if it is a sign.

# ...Nothing special"

"Before you attain it, it is something wonderful,
but after you obtain it, it is...

~Zen Master Shunryu Suzuki, about
enlightenment

# Nothing Special

Blood vessels are the same as sand by the tracks.

Also palms.  All God did
was make a leaf.


The tip-toeing child
reaching for the treat

he's not to have or quietly padding down the hall

late—if I have to say something


I'll say tree, I'll try out the myriad manifestations

of *the one*, like a hat in a hat


shop
I'll try on a bunch

but in the end they're all just hats.

# Reluctant Prophet

Wait for the morning to come

when no alarm clock is needed

to be covered in language and the blankets of nomads.


Now picture a hillside


dressed in dandelions, in Morocco.  There, you see a man


with a donkey,
he is Truth, they all are Truth.

*I wouldn't want to have too much*
*of a following,* he says, *because then I would have to lead.*


•


Like all else a critic
could call more than today's date
arbitrary:

the flying of birds in their patterns,

the pivot of the pilot in his seat, dodging the air
that pours through
his plane's broken windshield—

monstrous order,

arithmetic of fear,

geometry of divine paranoia,

every single life begins Once upon a time

and ends
*so and so* died on *fill in the date*—

•

Say to him, Expectation is a corset

making
you into your destiny.  While

to exist
is to be made whole

under the cloth of sleep
and a fragment

atop the daily sentence of wakefulness—hope

you wake with morning.


Like the jagged rocks of the middle school experience

every action leaves an impression
on what's to impress.

•


You watch him adjust the bridle of his donkey.
After a while, pointing he says

*Across that bridge is land and across it
is another bridge—*

*inevitable bridge, how could we ever
get across*

*the river without You? We, the boatless.*

# Wake

The room is full of flowers,

the flowers are on the wallpaper,

they subsume the walls into flowerness,

there is a person watching the flowers,

I watch the flowers.


Tomorrow, thank you for existing.


So many people are waiting in line, so many people

for all eternity are waiting,

so many waiting people.

# Fatalist Theme Song

It may be so
you can live anywhere you want

but the singing by one person to another
as he or she stands

beneath the balcony
seems suited to particular romantic locations.


But how can it be so
since to choose one way

is not to choose another,
thus leaving stones unturned, routes unexplored…


Bad dreams and their theories
all come in pairs: the horoscope

that led you to fulfill the wishes
of the bodies of the sky,

you swinging from the rafters like you
are the world's first monkey, named Lao-Tse, or Paul…

# Ghosts

And when they wake, and drag their hands across every unlit surface

And when they dream they will

It is a question, but by considering it we can whisper amongst ourselves
*what it is like to live forever.*

•

There is evidence of monks
who meditate on the fieriness of breath

to warm their bodies even in freezing temperatures.
Then perhaps it is so

we can separate the body into parts and say
I am not this, I am not this.

All because of concentration and what we could call consciousness

grappling in the halfway land or is it
all the way?

•

Things would be different
if the end hadn't come, when there was too much choice and not
      enough


Being: of all the poems in the world please let just one figure it out.

# Connection

The seawater sloshes relentlessly
against the green pier, calling *God* under its breath, *God,*

*God, God,*

and nothing changes.

I have a feeling
if I moved
even a bit of it—

if I could move—

it would be like the loose thread on an old argyle sweater

which, pulled, sends
the sweater

spiraling into non-existence.

# Punchline

The Proof now
is the Proof then,

in the ringtones of college students, the darning
needles of grandmothers

and the lawnmowers and skillets of everyone in between.


It's in the paws of otters and the bisected hooves of elk,
in the fantastic strength of lizards
and giant brains

of sea mammals, in the determination

of sharks and the sleekness of their movements, so decisive,
and the perfection of a bird's chest feathers
up close

and when they seem
a whole effortless mile above the canyon.


It's in the intensity of even the smallest stones

and the wizened immensity of two

thousand year old trees who, you wonder, are their tops
above the clouds?

It's in the soil and the fire's
inhale and exhale,

in the wait for the subway
who rockets us from one life to the next, and our impatience,

sullenness, joy, and pride,

in the suffering of the faithless and guilty
who ride out the minutes alone,

in the cockroach that is legion

over eternity—and in the certainty of the pious
who cradle a child
from within the fury of happiness,

it's in their tears.


And
it's in the punchline that is all our being and all our seeking—

these are
the roadsigns of proof, the victory of one definition

over others, the abstract
absurdity of living, here, wherever this is and why.

# Mosquito

Ancient insect into the muck.  To be a fossil

for the future billions,
the end of the tune
lingering in your ear:

*Will you wake up?  Have you ever?*

•

Stories we've all heard before but will hear again,
a simple description of happening:

it is dusk,
the sound of birds
mingles with an interstate
which for its own sake
is a kind of graceful separation, a pile of brush
and black-eyed susans
who look like sunflowers but are not.
Rosemary is in the air, concrete
is not not-life, walking
nonchalantly across a rooftop
is one squirrel, another behind, plotting.

Mosquitoes, despised by all it seems,
are harbingers of misfortune
dealt the hand of Judas—
should they have our mercy?


The sky is darkening, the cats have claimed
their alleyways and now are resting,
eyeing each other
with suspicion and perhaps hope.


Before long it will be dark, and then light again.

A drawing of the sun:

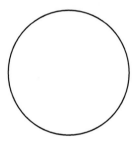

# About Gold Wake Press

Gold Wake Press, an independent publisher, was founded in Boston, Massachusetts in 2008 by J. Michael Wahlgren.

Titles:

Zachary C. Bush & Donora Hillard's *Covenant*
Kathleen Rooney's *Robinson Alone*
Andrea Witzke Slot's *To find a new beauty*
Kristina Marie Darling's *The Body is a Little Gilded Cage: A Story in Letters & Fragments*
Joshua Young's *When the Wolves Quit: A Play-in-Verse*
Erin Elizabeth Smith's *The Naming of Strays*
Evan Kennedy's *Shoo-Ins to Ruin*
Kyle McCord & Jeannie Hoag's *Informal Invitation to a Traveler: Letters between J.R. & Miss Kim*
Megan Martin's *Sparrow & Other Eulogies*
Nick Ripatrazone's *Oblations*
T.A. Noonan's *Petticoat Government*
Eric Beeny's *Of Creatures*
Kristina Marie Darling's *Night Songs*
Donora Hillard's *Theology of the Body*
Zachary C. Bush's *The Silence of Sickness*

All Gold Wake titles are available on Amazon.com, Powells.com, BarnesandNoble.com, and via order from your local bookstore.

# About the Author

Nick Courtright writes words and will have more of them someday. His work has appeared in journals such as *The Southern Review, Boston Review, Kenyon Review Online, The Iowa Review*, and many others, and a chapbook, *Elegy for the Builder's Wife*, is available from Blue Hour Press. He's Interviews Editor of the Austinist, an arts and culture website based in Austin, Texas, where he teaches English, Humanities, and Philosophy, and lives with his wife, Michelle, and son, William.

Feel free to find him at nickcourtright.com, or write him at nmcourtright@gmail.com.

# PUNCHLINE

CPSIA information can be obtained at www.ICGtesting.com
Printed in the USA
LVOW081136040613

336843LV00002B/86/P